# FLORAL MANDALAS

## COLORING BOOK

## VOLUME 3

This book is printed on just one side of the paper
to avoid bleedthrough.

To view samples of these illustrations colored by the author please visit
www.lovelyleisure.me

CONTACT: paula@lovely-leisure.com | 714.910.8998

## LOVELY LEISURE

### ILLUSTRATIONS BY PAULA PARRISH

Floral Mandala Coloring Book, Volume 3
© 2015 Paula Parrish

www.lovelyleisure.me

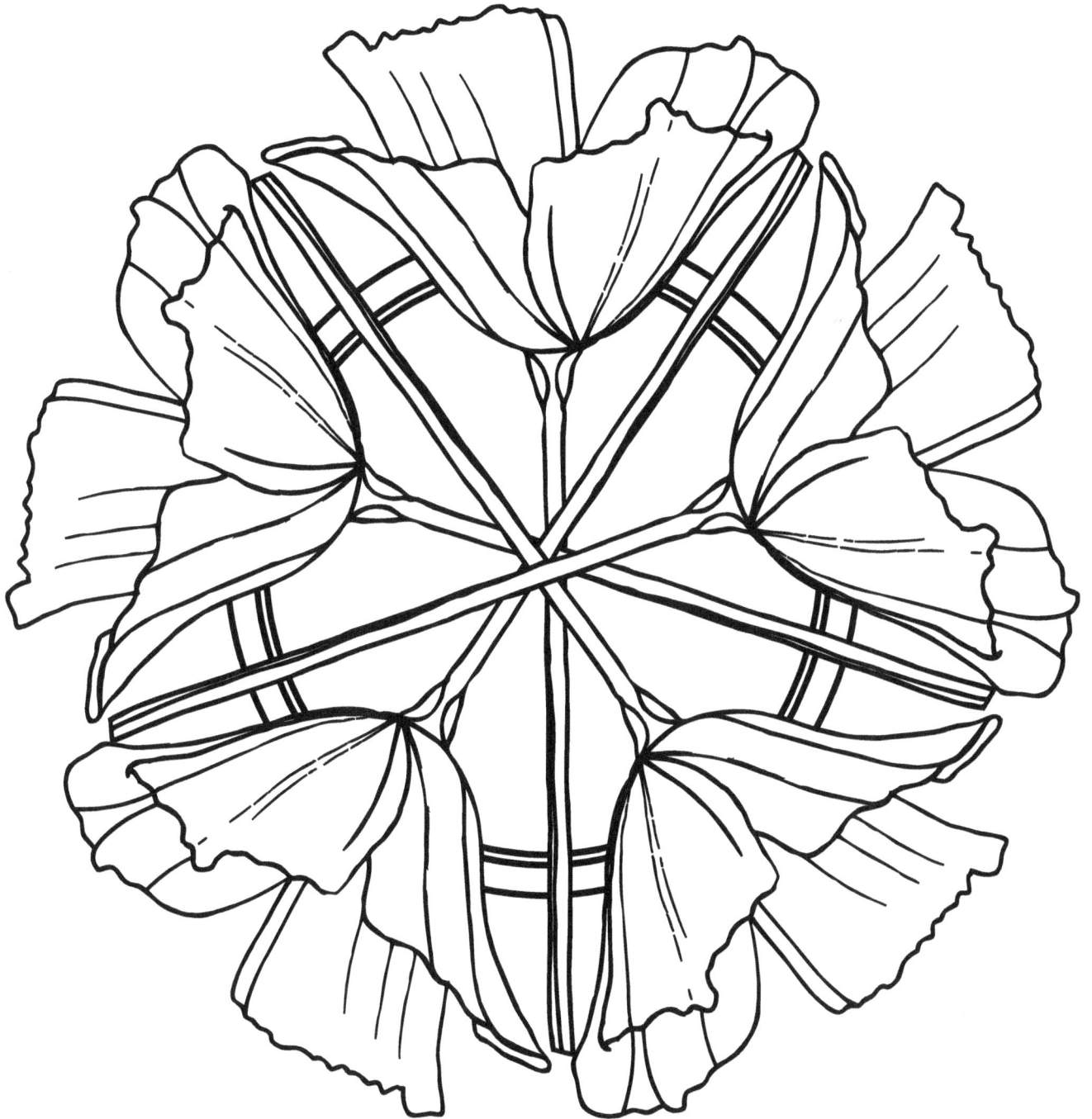

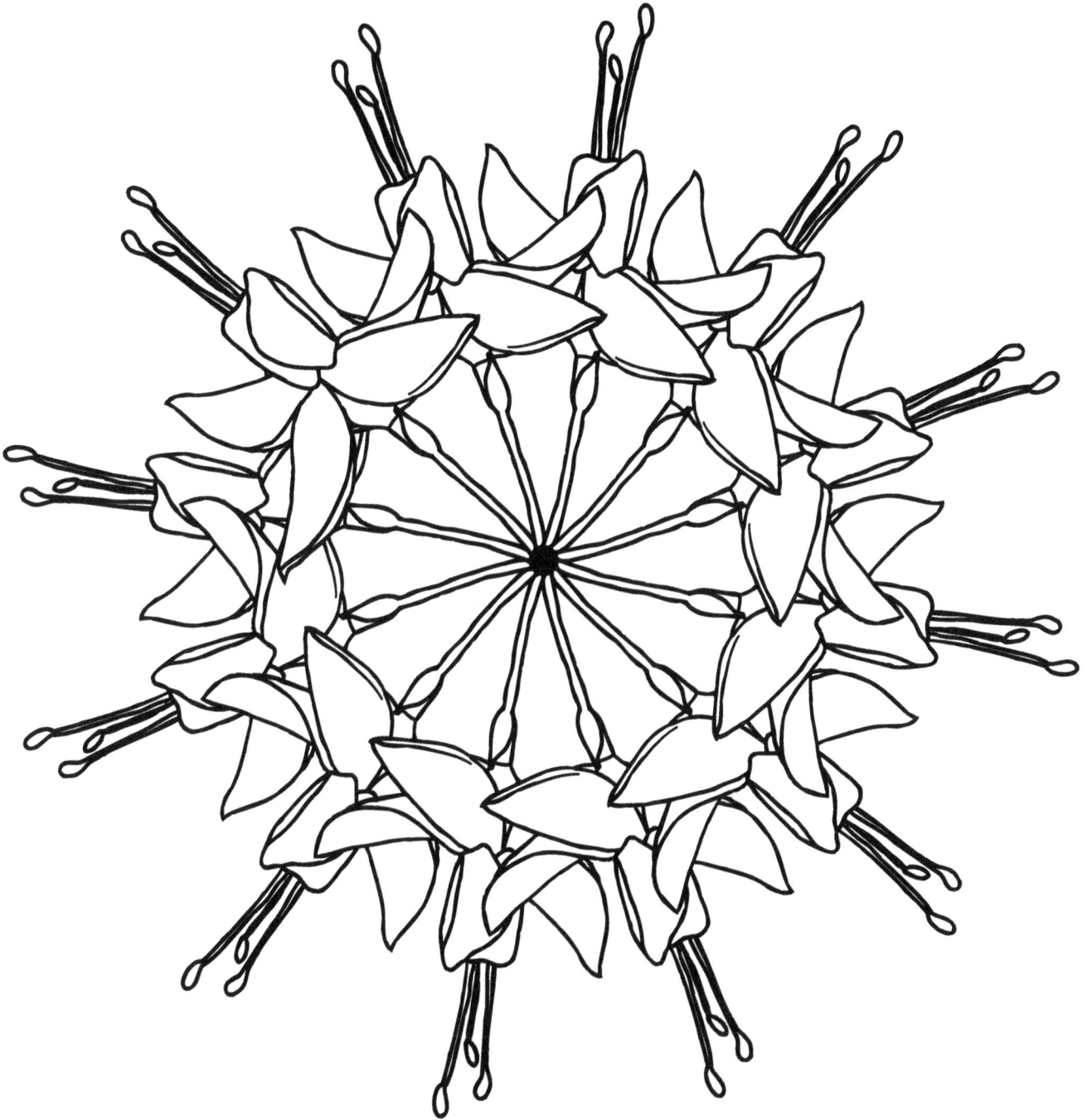

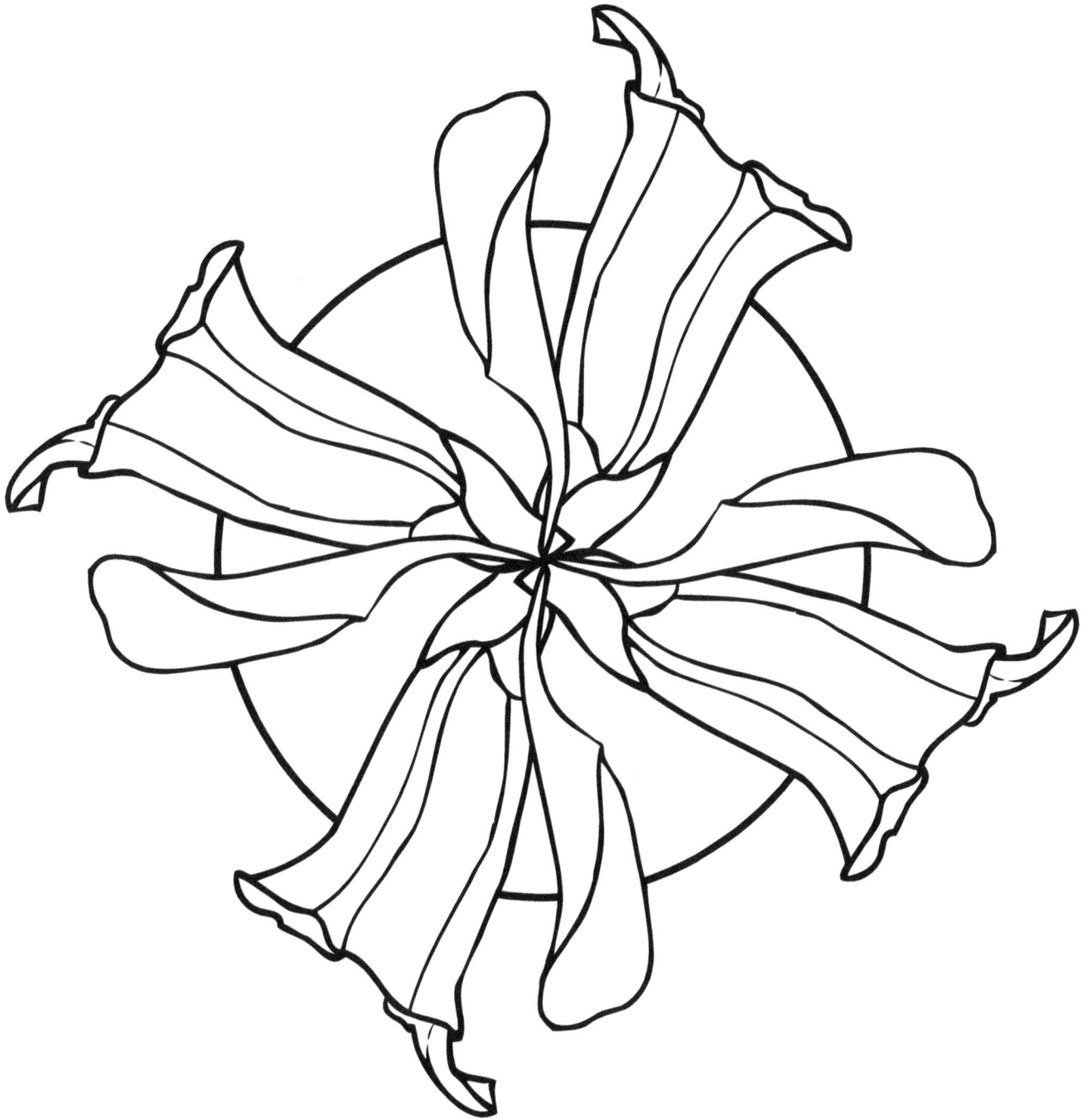

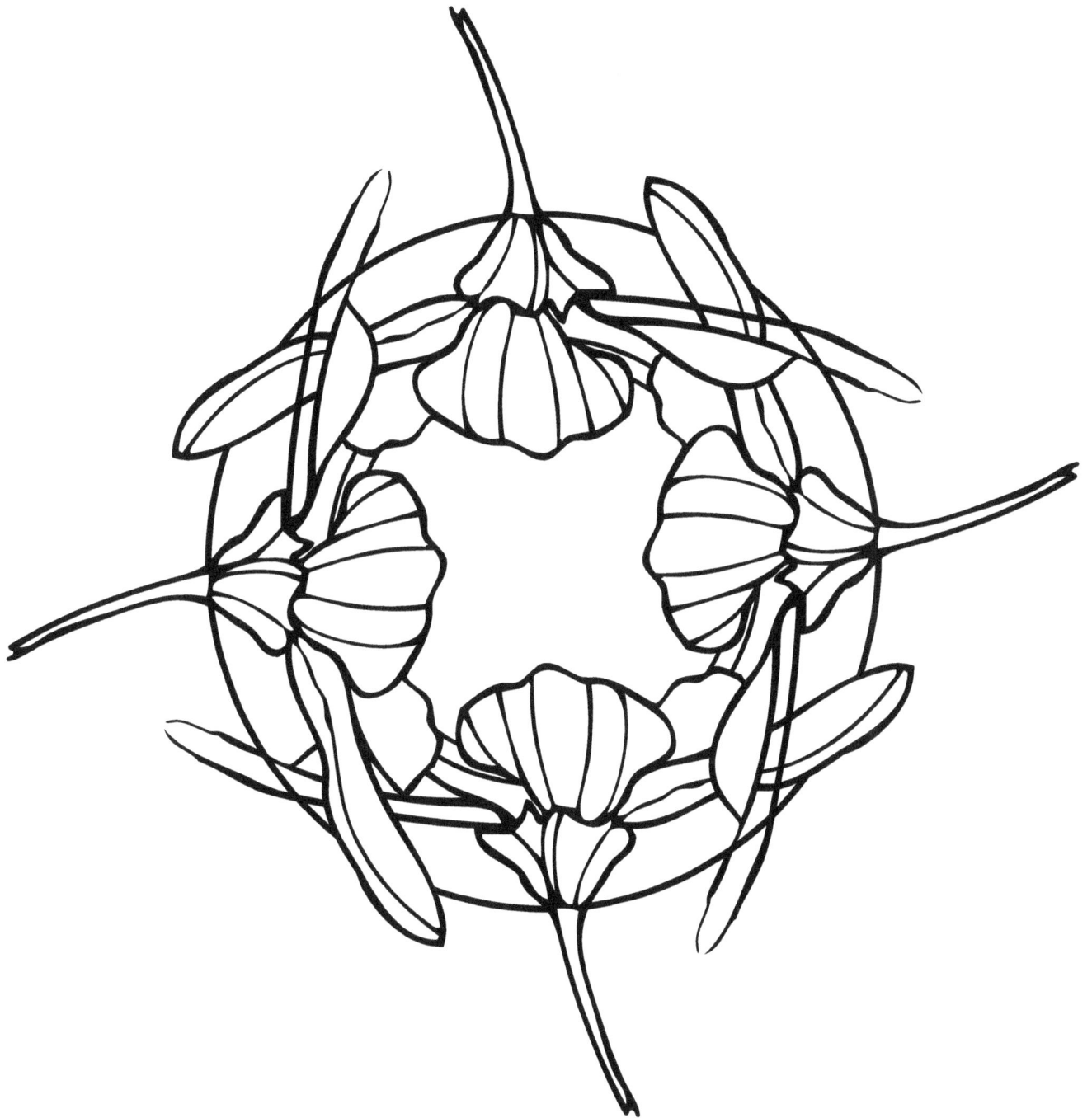

# COLOR SWATCH TEST PAGE

Use this page to test and reference your colors

Floral Mandala Coloring Book, Volume 3
© 2015 Paula Parrish

To learn about current and upcoming books,
and view colored samples of the works container herein,
please visit the author's website at:

www.lovelyleisure.me

www.ingramcontent.com/pod-product-compliance
Lightning Source LLC
Chambersburg PA
CBHW080528030426
42337CB00023B/4666